MW01223803

For Cynms,

Among Pearls Hatching

An amazing woman!
I'm so looking
forward to ~~visiting~~
seeing your
memoirs!

all best, Diane

Among Pearls Hatching

poems by
Diane Averill

DANCING MOON PRESS
NEWPORT, OREGON

Among Pearls Hatching
copyright © 2011 by Diane Averill
All rights reserved

No part of this book may be used or reproduced or transmitted in any form, or by any means, electronic or mechanical, including photocopy, recording, or any information storage and retrieval system, without written permission from the author, except in the case of brief quotations embedded in critical articles or reviews.

The scanning, uploading, and distribution of this book via the Internet or any other means without the permission of the author is illegal and punishable by law. For permission, address your inquiry to Diane Averill: **dianeaverill@aol.com**

ISBN-13: 978-1-892076-86-1
Library of Congress Control Number: 2011920432
Averill, Diane
Among Pearls Hatching
1. Title; 2. Poetry

Cover photo by Diane Averill
Cover design by Jana Westhusing, StudioBlue West
Book design by Carla Perry, Dancing Moon Press
Author photo by Molly Bellman
Printed by LazerQuick of Newport, Oregon
Manufactured in the United States of America

DANCING MOON PRESS
P.O. Box 832, Newport, OR 97365; 541-574-7708
www.dancingmoonpress.com
info@dancingmoonpress.com

FIRST EDITION
8

Acknowledgments

Some of the poems in this book have been published in the following magazines: *The Bitter Oleander, The Bloomsbury Review, Calapooya, Calyx, Clackamas Literary Review, Hubbub, Midwest Quarterly, The Oregonian, Pemmican, Poetry Northwest, Portland Review, The Oregon English Journal, South Dakota Review, Stone Table Review,* and *Tar River Review.*

Poems have been published in the following anthologies: *Beloved on this Earth: 150 Poems of Grief and Gratitude,* by Wesleyan University Press, *Deer Drink the Moon: Poems of Oregon,* published by Ooligan Press, and *Ravishing Disunities: Real Ghazals in English,* published by Wesleyan University Press.

A few of these poems have been included in my chapbook, *For All That Remains,* published by Fir Tree Press, and one in *Turtle Sky* published by 26 Books.

I would like to thank the following people for their suggestions on early drafts of these poems: Molly Bellman, Linda Cheney, Kate Gray, Jim Fleming, Pamela Gonsalves, James Grabill, Verlena Orr, Paulann Petersen, Susan Mach, Ron Talney, and Bill Siverly.

Other books by Diane Averill:
Branches Doubled Over With Fruit
Beautiful Obstacles
For All That Remains
Turtle Sky
Ella Featherstone Poems: A Sellwood Sequence

For my dear husband, Gene

Contents

Migration

Earth Choreography

Creed of an Unrepentant Pagan

I believe in the resurrection of forests,
the sanctity of solitude,
and the communion of crickets and humans.
I believe in the preservation of frogs,
their skins so different
from our own outer layers,
wet, more
like the skins of vaginas.
I believe in god the brother
and in god the sister
doing her angelfish dance.
I consider the word holy and the word sexual.

I study the power of green and yellow
and the holy spirit of blue.
These are the powers of the child who died
because he drew a picture of sky
and forgot to draw the sun.
I believe in art, not as pinnacle or pedestal
but as a way to breathe with your ribs expanding
the way branches of any winter tree lift
around their bird hearts in the wind.

I subscribe to the tease of my own ignorance,
the way it allows me to know.
I know the laughter of twelve-year-old girls on a bus
who can't stop themselves from laughing
faster than freeway traffic despite the turning
of adult frowns in their direction.
And I believe in young men who double up laughing
so hard they become one laugh.

I believe in the one god
of wildness, in the preservation of possums
and in the divine commandments of dream dragons.
And I know that the doctrine of dogwood
shadows the immortality of fireweed.

I practice release from instant religion,
from worship at the golden arches of Self.
I believe in the consciousness of all creatures
and I know that spider webs under my mailbox
receive messages from the morning sun.

I believe in the rainclock ticking on my roof.
Clearly the eyes of my brown dream
animal were the eyes of my grandmother
and I know a multitude
of blue-green leaves died and came back to life
in the eyes of my granddaughter.

1 know and believe that the raccoon's
watch-jeweler fingers sort through the garbage
of our civilized minds.
I learn from the long trail lit
by lantern leaves in the early fall
of humanity. I believe in sin
of omission, which is a tourist turning
his back on the deer that walk the spine
of Hurricane Hill because
Deer don't photograph well.

I believe in ethereal grasses and orgasms.
I know that time is a wave
of blackberry bushes rising
over a weathered fence wearing
flowers of summer foam—
whole minutes of them.

I listen to the different dialects
of pine and cedar and believe
in burning sadness to the ground
even though it will spring back.

I know there is prayer,
a red geranium lifting its many red heads
to the firmament, and I believe in sky,
a river of flame so fluid
a child could skip stones along its back.
I know and believe in the roots of this flame,
reaching deeply into the earth
to bring forth salal and salamander.
I receive the pulse of water
in the depths of Lake Crescent and I watch
the galaxies on its surface. I know
the little round ball of moss in the Hoh Rainforest,
peaceful as a lightly formed fist in
sleep is another kind of prayer.

For a Two-Year-Old Painter

Blue, slung in curves across the easel,
returns to her mouth in a berry-grin.
Naked turquoise belly. Hands,
arms, thighs covered in sky.
Paint dropping on the ground.
And then my granddaughter
flings into my arms,
a seedling from the wind,
settles on my hipbones
like a young tree
taking nutrients from a nurselog.
And I am crumbling, reddish,
spattered with beautiful blue beetles,
blue-green leaf-lace, moss-light.
My granddaughter grows from light
falling down on us like teal rain
and I know the forest canopy
will open for her into a sky
so blue she can see up through.

Earth Choreography

Sleep is a kind of soil dance, sometimes
when your moss-governed limbs
remember the chords of wind.
Then, there are reggae colors around the core of sleep.
Light and hair can fly.

In the soil-dance, feet leap around
angel-wing mushrooms and orange mushrooms
and mushrooms shaped like sea-star penises.
You don't know what all of them are called
during the day, you forget what
your abstinence instructor
said about which are poisonous, and you don't care
because their slower dances so gracefully synchronize
around your quick moves.

In soil-dance sleep, lungs gambol inside ribs,
air runs down canyons.
There is a lifting, a waving of leaves
that come from people you know died long ago:
lit flames of birch leaves surviving
the coal-white bark.

When you dance in soil-sleep, squash seedlings
come up to greet you, writhe like snakes
across your slumber garden
even as slugs move to write in silver calligraphy.
At the same moment, crazy
azaleas swing blooms across late November
near the white costumes of fan-dancing Pampas grass.

Sleep can be a blue morning glory window, so clean
it clearly seems to have disappeared,
so there is no barrier between your
self-dancing and squash blossom fire-dancing
or the ground-dancing around this particular sun
in this particular galaxy.

You become the shovel
and the dirt, leaping.
You wear leaves instead of clothes
in winter, in front of the memory woodstove
of your most prescient thoughts. You know your thoughts
are only seeds beginning their tango.

Garden Thinking

An apple tree planted years ago
sends out white messages
about a boy from Japan who ran inside
the first time he saw snow in Oregon,
thinking it a kind of dust,
thinking it would suffocate.
And as another shiver shifts the apple tree,

more white messages float down
the dreams of snow a friend has just before a relative dies.

In the garden it's impossible
to hold a death grip on any idea.
Thoughts irrigate the mind,
one enters another as the image
of a neighbor boy years ago holding
cut glass up to the yellow glint of noon
travels from morning news of
machete deaths in Zaire.
I dig out thistles.

After sifting the soil, careful
with thoughts that may burrow like earthworms,
I replace their twisting from my palm
back into wet earth, right
beside the candy-pink petunia,
which is too perfumed,
uncomfortably sticky,
like the voice of the insecure
high school girl I once was.

Older now, I know watering the lewisia
that levity needs good drainage
and fireweed should be
left alone to lighten the mind,
which is a compost pile laced with eggshells.
I know it is here
in the garden I can listen
to the day lily as she begins to speak in tongues,
and it is here I can begin speaking again.

Ghazal

In fall woods-water, a woman tastes sleep of leaves.
Father's green death-eyes closed in a waste: sleep of leaves.

Like koi, the red-gold of maples swims in wet grass.
She wishes fish would not be in haste: sleep of leaves.

Her baby's sweat smells of milk: rain clings to the fern.
Nursing, baby curves into the chaste sleep of leaves.

Seed-winds play with her baby's dandelion hair.
Seed-play can't reach her father's sleep of leaves.

Absorbed in poems, her baby's cry pulls her out.
Diane can't live for long in the laced sleep of leaves.

A Few Little Questions

i.
A low tock tock tock,
and I'm looking up to a woodpecker,
black and white where I expected color,
as in an old film.
The bird jumps to what's left
of last winter's ice-storm branch.
Now the tock of destruction
has a higher sound,
a different percussion.
Why is this new sound so like
my dead father's living room clock?

ii.
When the cerulean blue insect folded its wings
on the almost-transparent poppy petal,
it seemed as if it was resting
on a small piece of the sun.
But now, in the blue spring dusk,
the poppy has folded
its petals like insect wings.
So where have the real wings landed?

iii.

Last summer the cosmos
I planted in too much shade
turned the corner of my house,
reached with large stalks
for the sun, found it,
raised its many flushed faces upwards,
and warmed me with beauty.
In autumn, I plucked its hollow, dry stalks
and burned them in my woodstove,
where the cosmos kept me
warm a second time.
Who said the universe
is never kind?

The Cruelest Month

April sends late afternoon
sun snaking through new
leaves while feathery shoots uncurl.
I bend to a fallen willow branch,
see something once
alive, a little bone face,
bird claws still
gripping hard as life
that slim whip,
though its body is now
a weedy pod
emptied by time.
A maple leaf I'd forgotten to rake
last fall sticks tight
to feathers remaining.
Trying to unpry
my thoughts from the tiny
sockets turned my way
I carefully place the willow bird
in the trash bin
along with gray dandelion moons—

except for one. I wave it
in the quick breeze,
let it come apart in seeds
with silver wings.

A Sudden Awareness of Aging in Spring

From the slightly open window
there's a bell-like zing
as if a presence slightly
familiar from another life
has just touched the hair
on my bare arms. I hover motionless
over the cooling dish water
as Spring's first hummingbird
finds my feeder. It backs away from me,
becoming a red jewel in my blue morning.

I take chipped red dishes
from the drainer, place them down on
the wooden table, their plain music my control.
But when I look outside again
the day has turned against me,
gone grey. My hands are two crows
covering my eyes
as evening slowly reaches for the sky.

Beginner's Luck

The autumn we're eleven,
we keep our clothes on even
after we make a mattress of leaves.
He, on top of me for
a first kiss. *The edges of your body glow*
my voice tells our doubled self,
as he gently pushes up, away,
and I feel like an imprint he's made,
a snow angel in flaxen leaves. I spread my
arms, wave up and down in the fallen
needles and other, softer tree feathers.

After that I trust him
to carry me safely
on the handlebars of his bike.
He weaves in and out of puddles,
makes intricate designs with
newly wet tires
on the hot parts of pavement,
and though sometimes he spreads
his arms wide, we never crash.

One evening together in
a tree house abandoned by someone
too far past childhood,
we sit cross-legged.
Opposites: mirrors.
We've slipped by the witch's house,
gone further into the forest
than her hungers.

Flashlights under our chins
bring us new faces.
It's these beings who hum
in perfect pitch, who next shine
flashlights into our fists. It looks as if
our hearts have migrated into our hands.

I'm not sure,
looking at the backside of my skin,
through a beam of light strong as a shooting star,
if the webbed twigs inside
are the larger, hidden
finger bones, or if they're the ropes
that weave in and out inside my heart.

Then he waves his new hand,
A red flag for you, he says
across that tree house,
up and down
the border between our bodies.

When our hearts change
to red hot coals,
we're afraid we'll burn
down the forest. We don't know yet
that they're just signals,
know that our hands are our hearts,
that we don't know who we've become.

Before and After,
A Moving Point

Sun ambles toward a maple leaf,
touches its grooves,
travels, swings through it
as a woman moves with her lover across the blues
though he's in a plane,
and she is still on a green swing.
Her thoughts alight as his jet touches down
in the land of the Singing Revolution,
where a whole people
turned invading tanks around
with the united softness of music.

The pastor next door thinks music
belongs in his church: shut up.
The pastor is burning every plant, every tree
on the ground behind his house.
She let hers be, threw hair, loosened from brushing
into her yard of yarrow, firs, and trillium, for nests.
This helped bird song along. Now, notes
rise above thorns, stir the chorus of white
blackberry flowers. This tangle's her own
singing revolution.

The pastor's uprooted bushes
in front of his house, though she didn't catch
the point. *Too untidy*, he'd stated. She'd said
nothing, turned back to her green swing
where wilderness whispered to her,
as a whole tide of green swelled against the fence
built by someone who'd lived here before.
They'd gone on now, as this light has gone on
entering another maple leaf
and she wonders where her lover's singing this afternoon—
somewhere on the island of Saaremaa.
She recalls the whorls of touch in his fingers,
knows there is no point in love
that marks before, or after, only this steady
cicada hum, only whorls hidden in trees,
their secret marriages.
And light, the voice of song,
returns her to a younger time, turns her to
her first red cycles, and she hears again
that music, way back, telling her to let it be
the way it was before.

selfishness

I could sit on this pond rock
for as long as it takes
to fly to New York.
But is there a need
for so much greed?

These sun-warmed raccoon bones,
polished by birds and animals feeding,
then washed so clean by the seasons.
I hold them without fear.
A low chime when touched together.
I could stay here forever
as muscles relax,
my sitting bones reaching deeper
towards the earth.

Bird Memories

Your light-boned hands
migrate to me like birds.
Outside my body the vine maple sings
and soon all those good green motors, the trees,
start up and move through time
until evening brings light to closure.

There are many species of birds
in all hands,
and all hands sing,
though some are not in tune with time.
Some heavy bird-hands nest in laps like over-pruned trees
forced by manners not to fly. This, too, brings closure.

In the trees, some memories move like birds
who will never find closure,
that peaceful nest, even with time.
Some memories send bird-claws into scars along trunks of trees,
trees tapped too often by those who need lacquer to sing
because stones are what they think they have for hands.

The man who dropped the bomb on Hiroshima had the time
to taste its lead as it flew back to him like a terrible bird.
He will always remember this. He will never have closure.

And neither will the Japanese whose memories are trees
growing around the rubble of relatives who no longer have hands
to lift and sing.

My friend whose father's hands
hit her like falling trees
in the lightning storm that sex sings
to us all will never have the luxury of closure,
though she's tried to tame those neon birds
of memory through time.

If some happenings are not forgotten birds
knocked into the windshields of time,
what then is closure?
Is it the absence of a presence in the trees?
Is it memory migrating from hand to hand
in the form of pain that sings?

Your bird-hands turn and return to sing
of memories slashed and burned through time,
not always of trees or beautiful closure.

Horse, Iris

A white horse stretches its long
Neck into the wet green.
The brown horse walks slowly
Towards me like a wave, building.
I hold my breath. He hesitates, then
Stops. A rabbit softly bounds
Through the woods, hides by a fence post.
I continue my walk past irises
Streaming through purple beards
Like the manes of horses, stems long like the legs
Of horses.

The Oldest Story

Fir trees under the wind's power
spin in robin's-egg blue air
as my daughter contracts, pushes,
contracts. Screams. Pushes.
I am driving fast towards her call.
Gray moves in, blocks my vision.
Rain; then, a silver opening
parts the cloud's vaginal veil
and for a moment the sun emerges,
a fine sign. The sky is the blue-white of milk.
Remaining clouds rimmed placenta-red.

I arrive in the slipping-out time,
hold her in my hands,
body an orb half-covered in womb-white.
Body that has shed her red, jellyfish home.
First cries are lamb-like.
Next come me-ows as eyes shut to light,
then open again. Her hands are birds.
Mottled legs kick   Curl   Kick   Curl
as her petal tongue tries out the world's
will to listen. Then she turns
towards the answering voice
that sang to her in the womb,
and she knows that voice.

I give her back
as is my daughter's wish,
give my tiny granddaughter to that voice
that echoes from thirty years away.
Again, a cry has split me
as I place this glowing body
turning celestial-pink
into arms strong as fir limbs.
At Laura's breast lips grasp
the nipple's ancient wisdom—
and Natalie pulls the universe into her mouth.

A Field

The animal
inside my body
leaps over
whatever bends in her
path. Blue streaks
across the sky,
a far cry
from yesterday's clouds
where the only blue
jaywalked my feeder.

Here, dew turns everything
into small, multi-colored lights.
I look closely at sea-blue clover,
find the perfect glowing of a
web where the spider
zippers to the flailing moth.

Wild Grasses

Grasses caught
For a moment
In a bouquet on my oak table
Let loose
Lavender seeds on the yellow
Centers
Of the hope-filled dandelions.
A field is what
Grass wants to be.

Another Side of Desire

planets and stars

When we are
through the seismic shifts,
shared tongues and touches,
entering and reentry,
we come back to the world
we have left wondering
why the pictures are still on the walls,
why the roof has not
blown away by acts of god.

We come from orbiting
each other's bodies
like planets
around untouchable suns,
magically touching the unbearable.

We become friends again,
naked in mind,
the seismic shifts, subtle changes
in conversations that trust
the other will go where we hurt,
not build roadblocks of words,

still touching here
then there, hands, hollows
between legs, and genitals that need
to be walked like horses
after a race,

both of us winners,
holding high
golden cups that are
empty now, but ready
to be refilled
whenever we choose to be
together again.

Streaming

Her grief voice carried
steady tears along the trail,
spilling over for her old friend
dying that day, daughters
clustered around.

Seeing clearly is not
as easy as it sounds.
A young man, strong and tensile
as a sapling moved
along the trail with
a walking stick. No—
a didgeridoo. He played for
her sadness echoing deep
off the ground
in low, surging waves,
dense layers close to the
forest floor, firm,
unbroken
even as he raised it upwards
making sound into silk.
Circular breathing keeping
the wild wide open
as the oldest daughter, Sophie,

held her mother's hand
and somehow we knew
this time of dying.
Seeing clearly became easier
as Nature took us into
disappearance, the nature of things.
Someone said, *There are salmon!*
There are salmon spawning!
as rocks turned into fish.
They were moving to stay
in place against the current,
males and females beaten
to white patches from their journey's
scent compass, coming
all the way from Alaska
back, called back to this
Oregon riverbed.

Females flayed at the gravel,
then males rushed in,
sending white spumes over
egg clusters
as we stopped breathing
and started over, many times

being not as skillful
as the player's
steady
circular
breathing—
the power of
the didgeridoo.

No Trespassing

We wanted to know what was inside
The old barn, nailed
So a child could barely squeak through.

Needles of hay-light squeeze in
Cracks in the slats.
What could this teach us about NO?

We could hear, but not see, boys
Moving about like owls in the dark.

Judy found the rope swing
High attached to rafters and laughter.
On top of the bales I let go and screamed,
Legs wrapped around the skinny rope-knot,
Tingling as I dove downwards.

Then, in the middle of the swing-ride,
The hidden boys' blood screams,
Their tall, wild echoes
Entering my body
Went straight to my heart.

Extreme Posture:
A New American Yoga

The Water Mind

With waterfall strokes,
the former wife and her new lover
paint each other, pleasure
racing down the hills of their bodies.
Into their paintings goes the just-turned-liquid snow,
and they shiver, become
green shadows, alders reflected in a river.

The Rifle Pose

The medical student had said his wife was too soft,
a typical art student.
He disagreed with her position
on gun control, believed murders can't be prevented.
See, that kid who killed two classmates
and wounded twelve others, also had a knife.

The Scalpel Pose

The medical student, now a surgeon
cuts his former wife's original art down to size,
and positions it, facing backwards in the new frame,
just in case she becomes
famous some day. It may be worth something.

The Suture Pose

The surgeon's new wife is young, but barren.
She gives birth to a line of pricey greeting cards
from fathers who've moved to California
These become all the rage.
The doctor holds on to his belief
that his former children are
tainted by the painters.
He sends cards to keep them
away.

To a Sword Fern Frond

A little green finger,
you point something out to me.
What is it?
The strong July sun
creates a centipede beneath you —
but no, it's your shadow,
a temporary fingerprint
on the forest floor.

When I look from a new angle
you become Mother's sharp finger
pointing at me, the accused.

Too late, I realize
my human view's contaminated
with old mementos
as I'm invoked backwards
to sights glazed in memory.
I can't see you
for who you are. At least,
I do see that.

Reflection on Reflection

Lean, white
this log is all
smooth surface
now,
having traveled down
from a fir-covered mountain
to lay between rocks
just above Triple Falls.
Light-water beneath it
sparks the underbelly.
Water that is always
new, yet always the same
silks round rocks
covered in moss
velvet as peaches
that dropped easy as wishes
into my hands
the fall I turned woman.

But then this osprey,
on a twisty fir near the snag
where a great nest seems
to float like a raft
through late afternoon sky.

Her cry curves,
an urgent half-moon
above it. I look down
at the spill of thistle-glisten
at my feet, turn back
from all that is
not my life.

Her Eyes Say Rooms for Rent
(after Edward Hopper)

She stands before the window, or sits.
She looks beyond what the painter allows you to see.
The window is partially cloudy. Weather only.
Or the room is a sliver of city but she looks at something
Outside the stingy frame, outside of desire.

She's nude, sexy as a plaster cast, light as a light bulb
Unscrewed, and she isn't aware of you
Viewing a self helpless before the artist's brush.

The curtain says *come in* to the wind,
Says *stay away* to the viewer.
You want to leave, but you're helpless, too.
You're framed now
In another room. Like it,
You tilt slightly to the left, knowing that
Nothing can ever be right again.
Not sight beyond sight.
Not what the woman reads, or holds,
Or might do when you turn your
Now-vacant eyes back to your own narrowed world.

Offering

The autumn sky is an empty fruit bowl,
filling with clouds.
As my seventy-year-old neighbor offers pears,
I ask, *How old's your tree?*
We've been here 30 years, she says.
Like Mother, her answers never quite
match my questions.

The way to tell which pears are ready is
pulling gently, some will release in your hands.
I wonder how the green ones reached the grass.
If they ripen, they'll have bruises
where the ground hit them.
Other pears seem perfect. Looking closer, I see
tiny scratches like the ones my sisters and I
made on Easter eggs before placing them in dye.
Or like the patina our scared fingers made on bedroom walls.

Later, I water my impatiens before visiting Mother.
She talks of replacing the old
yellow sofa, sun-rotted from a huge picture window.
When she touches the fabric, it splits.
Mushy insides spill out; too far gone.

She knew everything. She knew nothing.

Now, she offers me her mismatched dishes,

hoping that will free her

to use her best. I have my own mismatches.

I refuse.

Longing for a Quill Pen

A person wants to write again
with a quill pen, feathers hovering
above fingers, dipping the tip
into an inkwell, to bring
that beautiful darkness up
into thought-words.

Bird energy would course through ink.
The bird's life would shadow through
the writing—

        its egg-tooth beginnings
        its flights
        its raising of the young
        its migrations
        its chill winters and lush summers
        its matings
        its escapes from cats and raptors
        and its final death.

All would be
there, as words take shape.
        A lawyer would try to write a brief
and the law would change, shift in wind.
        When a woman wrote a love letter,

pierced by a man's indecision,
that love affair might take flight,
then migrate back into the pen.
          When a child practiced her first letters
she would find everything but the truth
has flown out the window.

Meditations of the Displaced
Reaching Towards Wisdom

A person becomes anger for a while
but he is not anger. Anger has been
passed down to him in the fractures
of the abused woman who was
his mother, holding him in scarred arms.

Anger was in the air he breathed way back
in the uncurling time, air full of nicotine hate.
Anger in heirlooms woven into the ropes
of his muscles by a father who struck out,
by a grandfather who immigrated
to The Land of Disappointment.
                        A far wave of
Violence goes back   back,
                        diving into
a body long ago decomposed.
This was the soil he learned to walk on.

Violence composed itself into his body.
She sees it in his squinched face.
She hears it in the vile words, hurled at her
like illegal firecrackers.

She wonders how many times sweetness must sit at his feet
before he learns not to kick it.
How many times must innocence walk beside him,
a gold flower-face lifted up to his face
before he learns not to abandon it?
How many green limbs willow towards him?
How many openhearted anemones offer themselves?

There is no one like her. Everyone is like her.

The waves curl, uncurl. Her breath   the wind in pines,
her breath   black above ocean   her breath,
shivers of rain against the warm envelope of her back.
Breathe in   let go   breathe out   let go.

How many times can one breathe in
breathe out   breathe in a tide full of leaves.

Collateral Damage

Nests

Such slight pressure to pull down
a branch. Such quiet caterpillar sleep
in the weight of the not-yet-transformed.
Inside the silk, leaves have become brown,
though still attached to the branch,
while the ones outside and all around
are green waiting.

Each summer my father
set fire to the tent caterpillar nests
in our only apple tree.
Curled in that diaphanous womb with the others,
I wondered what I was like inside.
Lighting the kerosene wand, he smiled
as he smiled every evening.
I'd watch him through the picture window
when he arrived home from work,
Mother's threat curled inside my ears:
Wait till your father gets home.
By August we'd have perfect apples.

I think of this on a summer evening
as my lover's eyelashes give butterfly kisses.
As his hands come towards me
like wings that have migrated
all the way from some other childhood,
we share the body, that ecstatic, imperfect fruit.

Night Vision

Frogs mating under tulip-tree moons
Just beginning to open are shaped and colored
Like two old brown maple leaves.
For two years now I've heard them pulsing
In the pond but never seen. Each year they grow louder
As they multiply. Today I can walk right up to them
They look back at me, their four brown eyes mud.

It is raining softly here but across the world
Camouflaged soldiers wait out the sandstorm.
Exploiting camouflage borrowed from nature, they seem
Sinister. The frogs seem sinister, too, if you turn the corner
And view them under fluorescent light.
Claws like human fingers, the males pressing the female.
The soldiers wait restlessly, prevented from moving.
Only their blue eyes stare.
Here, the rain falls on this sustained union of stillness.
I back quietly away.

A Curse for Peace
(for Tormis & the Estonian People)

A spear, a cursed iron spear.
The music of anger, the sword.
A beat for peace.
A curse upon iron.

The answer is never
In the killing iron.
A curse upon iron.

A curse upon the wounds
Tearing songs into pieces of terror.
Turning red into voices,
blood dripping from iron's tip.

A curse upon the sword, the cannon, the bomb.
A cry for those captured, for those enslaved.
A curse upon wars
Where the lives of the dead
Rip the hearts of the living.
A curse upon iron.

A shout for the strong songs
That won't be silenced.
A cry for the grief in the drumbeat.

The drum answers war
With a curse upon iron.
The shaman drum made from the inside
Lining of Reindeer's urine.

The drum is the heart of rebellion
Yet the drum is the hurt.
It echoes songs like screams so strong

They appear without warning
In choirs across the world.

The shaman leaves no peace-heart unvoiced.
The drum lets no curse-beat go by.
The shaman keeps time
To the curse. The curse upon iron.

Out of Nowhere

i.
A hovering self holds
My arms over a stainless pail.
Ladybugs fly out of slit wrists.

ii.
I'm eleven years old again, swinging
My arms as I walk, when the heart
Charm on my bracelet
Suddenly snaps open into
A gleaming wasp.
I close it sharply.

iii.
Blood drops from the maple tree,
Stains the patio beneath my feet.

iv.
I watch crimson
Stripes on my neighbor's flag
Smear before my wet,
Red geranium eyes.

v.
A hummingbird sipping delicate blood
Inside my throat
Prepares for our long migration.

Nothing's Changed

Entering the stained glass
of the New Age Bookstore
I discover myself shopping
while televised screens aim at me
from each corner
and clerks imprisoned behind counters
made of endangered wood
and working minimum wage, no benefits
watch pricelists on ash-gray computers
for past-life autobiographies written
by former spiritual masturbators.
They occasionally glance at monitors
in search of pilfering prayer-hands.
God or goddess, the Omnipotent owner
is not visible.

Having transformed themselves from their
former dependencies on consumer culture
and the language of Christianese,
holiday shoppers   Being Here Now
are considering winter solstice
cards marked up 60 percent
and videos on simplifying their lives
(For ONLY $24.99!)

A woman in a handmade off-white dress—
the one who created celestial beings
glued to sea-shells—
bends benign dyed-blonde hair
over a customer buying one of her divination packets
to autograph the angels.

Meantime, an old man listening
to a meditation tape
removes the store earphones,
turns and says to his companion,
Sounds just like the old
Woolworth's Dime Store.
Ya know. The one with the
caged parakeets, and cokes clinking
on glass showcases.

The Pentecostal Locksmith

The door is closed, though
the sign says open.
It's a little square
in the center of the mall.
Inside, a huge poster shouts
PENTECOSTAL REVIVAL.
The picture shows
everyone's hands raised
as if they are participating
in a hold-up.
The automatic door slams shut,
as the man behind the counter
says he wants to help me,
I search for his eyes under smudged glasses,
think of fish in cloudy water,
I can't locate his pupils.
He hands me a postcard replica
of the poster from a stack beside
the cash register as I hand him my key.
When I say, *I believe*
we should concentrate on what all
religions have in common, like love,
like compassion, wrinkles appear in his forehead,
around his mouth, enclosing his words in a frown:

Love. Compassion. Our similarities won't
get us out of this earth. I think
of the huge pentecostal church
introduced into our neighborhood.
Like non-native grasses, its parking lot takes over,
the concrete pushing out what used to grow.
And in the center of the straight, yellow lines,
a metal speaker like a periscope
pumps twenty-four-hour church music
into the new lot.

Unfortunately, there's a lot of wrong
doctrine out there, the locksmith continues.
I recall the church's suspicion throughout centuries
of tritones, called *diabolus in musica,*
because they span three whole notes . . .
organized religion considers
dissonance dangerous. There is a monotone grinding
now as this man turns his back on me
to create my new key.

Arrivals

They wouldn't give us water at Auschwitz,
she says, as Dr. Epstein makes sure
she has a large glass of water at the podium.
Only a small barrel of it in the cattle cars
not enough for all and not nearly enough
on the ship from Rhodes,
and that tasting greasy, of olive oil.
And no water as we arrived at the camp
calling out for it, our tongues swollen,
stuck against our palates.

She arrived at the campus among hailstones,
Diana Golden, her hair slivering the day,
like strands of sun through clouds.
She was a little late,
yet in plenty
of time. *I was silent for 20 years*
after coming to
this country. Now I give
two talks a week. I must speak.
There are new books. They say
the Holocaust never
happened. After 50 years I still dream
they are coming to get us.

Hail turned to rain as we ran
between buildings to the students.
My thoughts ran along Diana's bright
blue coat as I listened to the professor
saying, *I'd like a grandson to carry*
on the Epstein name. Six million. Dead.

There were gypsies
at the camp, and homosexuals
and Jews from different countries.
We were all in separate buildings.
We spoke Italian, but it was the German girls
who died first.

In room 206 she tells us the number
on her arm, returns to the day
of Auschwitz arrival.
I remember standing there. Our clothes
taken from us. Only our shoes left.
Naked, but no one touched us
we were so filthy. Shaven, shivering
after the cold shower
turned off before we were clean.

No towels. Separated from our men.
An SS guard dressed, I remember,
in a blue skirt. Pleated. I remember the pleats.
She had on lipstick, she had hair.
She looked human. We weren't human.
We were vermin.

I look around at my students,
concentrating on her words.
Yet one leaves
for the drinking fountain,
another to the bathroom.
She is telling us
there were no bathrooms in the cattle cars.
A student whispers, *She skips around a lot.*
Why is that, I whisper back, *do you think?*

My fingers wrap around an electric blue
Starbucks cup. Now she is talking
about the young
bodies of women
she saw every morning; naked
they'd thrown themselves against the electric
fences   dying to pain.

I flash on this morning's news,
the woman with metal hooks for hands staring
at the rapist who cut off her forearms,
then freed, killed a woman.
And Diana is saying, *No one knows*
who can or cannot endure. There were 2,000 Jews
taken from the island of Rhodes. In the end,
only 130 survived. One hundred were women.
She goes on talking to us, goes on
over the newscaster in my head.
I skip around a lot, I think
as her words fall on us, fall around all of us,
arriving hard and clear as hailstones.

What Was Left of Me

Hardly any girls talked
In high school my junior year.
There were the *Hi's*
Sprinkled around halls,
The lipstick so pale
It looked like slug trails,
The girls in girdles
That kept us contained.
We tamed our hair at night
In scratchy, big curlers. Days we
Teased our hair and the boys.
The only two Jews at that school
Were my friends, the Goldsmith girls.
They kept silent about the Holocaust,
Even that day in U.S. History
When the woman who'd survived
Auschwitz showed us the numbers
Tattooed on her arm while we looked
Down at our charm bracelets.
She told of many that drank their own
Urine in the cattle cars, told of women
Who threw themselves upon wired
Fences, electrocuting themselves.

When the class bell rang, the girls
Flowed back into the narrow halls,
The *Hi's* still the only voices,
The lipsticks smiling.
I backed against a wall,
Could not enter the stream of bodies.
I made it just in time
To throw up again and again
To wind up on a cot in the office
Until my parents retrieved
What was left of me.

My Jewish friends maintained their silence.
I wanted to ask Susan and Beverly where their
Jewish names went? Why did some choose death
While others survived? Why were their parents
So happy? Where were their relatives?
But politeness
Shut us off from each other
Like barbed wire.

Of Mourning

At six I wake
To the dark
Re membering
The long drive
With my daughter
Because Mother has taken
A turn for the worse.
Red stoplights.
A convenience store
Where the clerk calls
My daughter, *Ma'am.*
When did she grow
So far?

At the hospital we
Round the corner
That is Mother's number.
Her number is up.
I fall into my sister's
Unshed tears,
Back out of that deep
Water. Mother's eyes
Can't close. Only her
Breathing is alive.

Her last words
Before the coma were
I need my compact
And my lipstick.
Putting her face on,
She always called it.
Told us *fix yourself up.*

Only up talk here,
Says my sister.
She may be able to hear.

My mother is centered in bed
Like a spider, all abdomen
And thin legs and arms.
Webs of tubing surround her.
Her once-rose skin tone
Rises to my eyes,
Grey now as a cloud
Above her skeleton face.

I lift the oxygen
Mask from her mouth,
Apply salve, give her
Back to the oxygen.

Her systems are all shutting down,
Says the nurse
As if my mother were a machine.
I want to take her
To a better place,
Where they could
Fix her up. No one can.

For My Mother,
Who Passed From Us in November

She took a breath, then no more.
Sisters, daughter and I dropped to our knees by her bed,
like cranes folding their legs,
symbol of peace in Japan.
Child-sized again, one-by-one,
we said a prayer for her.

Ashes

Soon Mother
Will be released
Into the ocean
She loved.

My mother's bird-lilting voice. Ashes.
Her proud backbone. Ashes.
My mother's body—that picture
Of her as a little girl floating
On the inner tube at Lake Superior.
Ashes. My mother's body old,
Twig arms and legs, organs slowly fading
Like a sepia photograph
Of 1918, the year she was born.
As it was in the beginning
Day of her life, her only struggle
Became breath.

Memory ashes of her calling me in
From play with a bird whistle
Fashioned only from her hands.
Laughter ashes.   Screaming ashes.

The warm past. The cold present.
Maybe now she is a seagull.
She always wanted
To come back to that path.
Maybe some of her ashes

Will find an oyster and
Become pearls,
Glowing and lovely again
Around the neck of a new woman
One pearl touching the pulse
Point at the throat which is light
Red as the scent of her perfume.

Burial at Sea

On the ferry between Seattle
and Port Angeles,
each of my sisters
holds a handful of Mother-ashes.
I hide in a seagull's eyes.
As they let her go,
grit and bits of bone,
I hear a voice
calling from a cell phone
in the ashy palm of
a sister's hand.
As I light gray and white
on the railing,
the sea becomes sun's summer
morning. My sister says into the phone
Mom is sitting here with us
in the form of a gull.
On the railing
the sea turns rose in the gull's eyes
and that's how I know this voice of mine
isn't really me at all—
my lips full of ashes
disappearing into water.

Shoplifter Hands

The ego's reach is so strong
that yesterday, when I thought
I was wise, even
in the beautiful fall
Camassia Wildlife Refuge
where I'd gone in reverence
for all that remains of the wild,
for all that still
exists of peace,
I watched my two hands

merging fast as cars onto a freeway,
coming together in a concrete motion
to lift a bird's nest
away from the chosen branches
as if it were only a trinket in the mall

as if emptiness could not be
refilled next spring. A quiet trill
pulled me over to the other side of desire
I lowered my arms, swayed
in the quickening wind.

Administrative Piece

Welcome aboard.
As we reposition ourselves
to meet the challenges ahead
we must remember to keep
our noses over the horizon.
Student success depends on diversity
while transitioning emergent proactive agendas.
The student is the customer, the outcome, base.
Remember to celebrate a sense of humor
while we empower ourselves
with fundamentally important learning tools
and high performance ideas.
The new technology demands it!
Think globally; act locally, for the power is with us.
However, as we explore new vistas of understanding
and meet the people, we must consider options for
budgetary adjustments which move our master plan
in the right direction. We have it in place.
We're ready to jump forward,
to take a serious run at this!
The engine for our future will help us
float some concepts here, today.
But this is only a subset of our values.
More than ever before,
you, the key players, will help us form close
partnerships as we move from visions to reality.

Please calendarize that. And let us know
how it impacts you. We've reenergized to keep
abreast of your ongoing concerns and
turn them to the best purpose
as we reshape education for the 21st century.
And don't worry. We have you
on our screen.

Collateral Damage

For two summers in a row,
unlikely deer stepped out of the tree farm
into a wild lot, ripe
Himalayan berries in their mouths.
Those blackberries were not
supposed to be there.
They're non-native. They take over.
And the deer weren't to be, either,
with lips around the growing tips of firs,
those nobles designed
for the little lives of Christmas.

But for two years the deer were—
I swear it.
They lived in that tree farm, in that blackberry dusk.
Spots of late afternoon sun along bark
turned into ears.
Shadows in front of fir became whole
gently moving bodies. And then? Erased
from following summers
as if drawn by a child
who'd later been taught symmetrical lessons.
The wild lot, the berries replaced
by carpet grass, electric fence,
an oil-smooth horse.

This Piece Removed from the Exhibit Due to Complaints Regarding the Misuse of Fruit Imagery

(sign found above a blank, white space)

The bolts remain,
and the white wall,
and the absence of misused fruit.

The watermelon whose insides
were scooped was seedless to begin with.
Not fair for us to view the green cave
that was all
the artist left.

And the cantaloupe has gone rolling
somewhere in the sky,
but the viewer shouldn't
worry. It's happier as the fifth moon of Jupiter.

Only the apple, discolored, bruised,
definitely misused, is to be
pitied. It hides its starry, black beginnings
from those who want it only for its beautiful gold skin.

Someone disliked how the grapes hung,
how they invited mouths
to cover their green nipples.

Before the removal of the fruit
there was no reason for guilt.
After the misuse of removal,
the fruit imagined its roots,
regenerated in other paintings
and hung itself
not in despair
but, yes, in secret.

All over the city, fruit crept
into other paintings.
Raspberry juice dripped from a watercolor brush.
Figs, peeled down to their inner chambers,
shrugged off one acrylic attempt
to cover them with their own leaves.

Arms blossomed. Artists marveled at their
originality as the fruit reasserted its origins.
Sculptures became fruit orchards,
producing cherries
even the most cranky of complainers
would not hesitate to keep
though perhaps disguised in pies.

Paint by Number

Well-endowed art
is safe art,
voluptuous, overfed.
No sick children
alone in rooms with chipped lead paint.
No hungry people, skinny as models.
What will the well-dressed sculpture
wear this year?

Well-endowed art
is the art of makeup.
Putting on my face,
a woman called it
when she had to paint to please.
First, a base
coat, stretched thin
across the skin,
then liberal use of the
cover-up stick. Botox those
unsightly frown lines,
get rid of tattooed tears.
No irregular, erotic brush strokes.

Well-endowed art
is white,
is nothing
wild or critical.
Straight as eyeliner pencil,
it's only colored between the guidelines.

    These stretch for miles across the minds of artists
    like ocean drift nets that tangle and kill.

shock

Your words continuously travel like caterpillars
From across the room towards me. I cannot hear
Them yet.

I'm moving out. Tomorrow.

My hysteria flowers. You reach for
Your best friend, Cigarette.

The day after disappears.

Now, I hear your words.

Hummingbird in a Rare Rainforest Setting on the Coast

Iridescent green moves among manicured rocks,
tulips that will never be
past their prime,
and seashells painted like toenails.
In this glass-eyed porch
of the costly bed-and-breakfast
nothing else breathes except
that which is attached to the frantic
wingbeats. Even though I'm here,
even though others are here,
I say nothing
breathes. Not the tiny, stuffed bears,
bearing price tags
on soft backs bent like croissants.
Not my overstuffed tourist mind,
which will, in a minute
try to change all this,
and fail.

Finding the Dark Time

Insubstantial now,
she lay down below fern,
leaf-shadow on a half-cloudy day.
Above, hail displaced apple blossoms,
filling the air with the scent of
white melting into moss
where a newborn
dinosaur-headed sword fern
began its soft uncurl.
Under her were the roots of fir,
seeking water, going as they must have gone,
step by rooty step
in their own decade-slow way
towards the marsh for centuries.

As sun came back she recalled the bones on rocks—
was it just this morning—
right above a veiny stream.
Bones of a small animal she couldn't name
because it was no longer dressed in a face.
Naked jaw's teeth serrated
like a sword fern. It was this that had
given her the gift of time
stopping for awhile, for long enough
to lay herself down.

Migration

Apple Light, Pine Mirror, Maple Coal

I cradle an apple, then pull down yellow,
raise it to the wriggle of autumn sun.
That night I sleep with trees. Green dreams
ignore glass panes, seek grass, find lightning-singed
branches that snake through anorexic moonlight.
Morning turns over,
falls and falls in the amnesiac winds.

Waking, I can hardly hear the pines,
though their faces are kind, kindled in
my mirrored wall. A branch knocks
against wood, like a friend
who wants me to come out and play.

Outside, I hold yellow babies,
old souls given to me by maple.
They shiver and shine, then hush.
Now I lay them down to sleep
among asters where incubus rain
takes care of their bodies. I abandon them,
knowing I can't be their good mother,
knowing below these blue stars a slower presence
can raise them to spring.

When dark grows pregnant, I move back inside.
My fire holds leaf-flame babies.
I wish for yellow palms, sing psalms to coals
to keep their warm bodies alive,
but my barren hands are full of smudged intentions,
and I can't touch light's echoes.

Woman Alone

It wasn't easy the night the man
who appeared uninvited beside my down comforter
was a composite of my ex husband and ex boyfriend.
It didn't reassure me when
he said, *Don't be afraid, it's only me.*
And it didn't help either when I had to duck
under the smoke-and-granite crumbling face
of my dead mother to get to the phone.
It was even worse when, after crying, *help*
into the drain-holes of the receiver,
the policemen showed up as
eels, shining their flashlight eyes
into every crevice of my house.
But when all they found were two bluebirds
nesting in my bedroom, I knew what I had
to do. Making the policemen leave
the birds' eggs where they were, I found myself
alone, and went to sleep among pearls hatching.

Bridges

She once was a well
Full of blue-white milk and now
That well is empty.

Her dry body walks
Along a braided stream
Where herons bring twigs

To quiet eggs
Whose nests are high.
The terror she crosses

Reminds her how easily
She could be erased.
Olive snakes flower the air.

They show her how to go
Slow over uneven rocks,
Stuttering across them

The way a bumblebee flies.
Finally, she kneels
Where water offers reflection—

Mallards pairing up disguise and color,
April turning its blue head in
A flicker tree before mist

Wipes it all out. Dark rains down,
Filling her up. Leaving,
Her fur sheds the extra water.

Wildflower Kiss

Touch of lips and beauty crosses over into fear
where pleasure pierces green pain needles. Tongue on tongue
overwhelms the human skin, becomes all wildflower meadow

and you are alone. On Hurricane Ridge, a kiss is not simple.
It beams light long after the descent, it is becoming tongues
edged with the blues of lupine further edged with reds

and each slight movement causes snakeweed to brush lips.
There are hard, icy crushed sandstone and shale
shoved together by a strange force moving against your bones.

When you kiss in the forest you kiss a crescent of lake water
and tongues are edged with paintbrush leaves,
colors wildly membrane moving. There is a dark bee

in that kiss, pulling over the fluted tips of the common
morning glory petal and you wonder why it is evening.
Storm King Mountain, black now, the sun having gone

behind it, lights up all waves, unending and increasing
speed because wind is in the kiss, and fish leap to catch you
in their mouths. This alarms you. And so do the alders,

arms and legs leaning so far over water you fear falling,
roots exposed. The cold mysteries of mountain peaks
are in the fingerbones holding you, a tiny blue moth,

in the trail-line and an eye, somewhere far off, is looking
down. It sees your tiny moth body, though you are blue
and try to disguise yourself on a lupine flower.

That flower shines through your skin. You know your life
is very brief, seconds only. In a Hurricane Ridge kiss
of flower to moth, you have a thousand eyes inside each eye,

you taste with your feet, and scent extends for miles
across wild meadows. The inside of this kiss
is wings breaking the air, white waves

finally drying after birth. The inside of this kiss
hovers above its bright food instead of quietly
hanging below a leaf, hoping not to be seen.

When you live inside a rainforest kiss, each moment
reveals the next, and you don't know
whether you are inside time as a circle of tree rings

or a circular spider web with the spider on her way
to greet you from the new strand she has just thrown
onto the tip of your tongue, a newly uncurled fern frond.

When you climb time, you could be on your way
up tiers of firs on a mountain or tiers of mushrooms on an
ancient tree. And sudden rain is not always water.

It can be high-pitched fir needles carried
by air currents down past ripe huckleberries to
hit the ground with dense sounds. You used to think only

rain could tock like that. Wildflower kisses are
pleasure, yes, but terrifying, yes, because your skin is
permeable, almost tree-frog chorus, almost mist.

Ramona Falls

is a young girl
wearing a white dress
and black, shiny shoes.
                  She's tripping gently
over
          uneven
rocks on a sidewalk,
her fan-like fingers
               touching down on
liquid-green grasses,
               her shadow rivering on
into the woman
        she's now becoming.

The Passing of Summer Time

The territorial sighs of widows
living in apartments with names like Summerplace
gather like bird wings in birch leaves.
Below those sighs
I hear smaller breezes
tearing the white wings off moth-flowers
that were covering the young
bodies of green berries.

As the ticks of hummingbird beaks against the feeder
mark minutes on the sweetness clock,
across the street there's a slap of small feet
as my granddaughter jumps from a swing.
Or is that a memory of the first wave I ever heard
as it hit the dock at White Bear Lake,
returning to me now as the sweet water
of the hummingbird feeder drops?

When the green berries ripen into black ones
they will add to these short nights
drop by drop, and then my daughter will be
listening hard.

Willow Tree Bird Dancing

Unwatched, she thinks,
my twelve-year-old granddaughter
dances the highest cliff above the ocean
throwing to the wind
the burdens of being young,
shedding the pink
camisole. She isn't Barbie anymore,
she's dips and swoons, now a gull,
long bare feet close to the edge of
a world which drops away
from the surf pounding
against the land
and up through her bare feet
and into her racing heart.

She pauses, one thin leg holding
all her desires, her heron-blue eyes
in love with the waves below.

She skirts the edge
like a ballerina on stage
as close to the rope saying
DO NOT GO BEYOND
for whatever reason
would take a dancer
soaring into space.

Her green arms lift in the wind,
transformations taking place so fast
she levitates in time and holds
while the crashing world below
waits out the touch
of her soft bare foot.

i.

Out-of-Body

Though dying when
I looked down on my body,
I could now   move freely.
It was exhilarating, like the first time
balancing on a bicycle,
like the first real swim.
I wanted to stay there,
to turn corners, increase speed,
go and go into this new move,
though my friend was calling me,
as a parent would when a child strays.
He was holding on
to my hand, a glove I'd misplaced.
Looking down at his bent head,
the top of his sorrow,
I decided to come back,
as a reluctant child
playing outside the boundaries would,
            turning around, dragging my new
feet slowly back home.

ii

Inside the Body

A shy snake lays its eggs
in the safety of my body heat,
hiding under composting thoughts.
Each egg is safe from eyes. Each egg
rests for now, as a full moon's reflection
on a windless night in unpeopled woods.

Inside my breasts, blue-white moon-threads
were pulled by the tides of my babies' hungers
long ago. Now, these threads form
the material of the birds' nests in my heart.

The tiny bones in my bird feet
try to fly. Sometimes, in the music
of Arvo Pärt, or Muddy Waters,
air feathers around me,
and they can.

In a Tree

In late December what used to be
a crabapple tree is now the junco tree,

though birds cling to branches
more briefly than fruit holds,

and in late December, wind
waves the last yellow

leaves next to snatches of fir branches
that arrived in the junco tree

yesterday on a beautiful storm,
on wind that blew my thoughts of this past year

far across town, where they held for
a moment, in the Blue jay-blues eyes of my daughter,

before passing through
my bright granddaughter, rippling in the limbs of her mother.

A Growing Whirl

The glowing galaxy of seed
Assumes gray perfection. Just as
The sun touches it

A tiny girl blows it apart
Where it floats beyond her,
Beyond the planted people of light

Green formality slipping their
Bent bodies into darkness,
Even though lupine spires

Open a blue wall in the girl's
Playhouse that allows
Passage to red
And back to a scary, dark lawn.

When next morning's
Apple-peel sun brings her
Out to the street,
She and her sisters
Soon grow old enough
To try to ride their brilliant bicycles.

The sisters' many tries
Stop with abrupt leanings
Until the final moment when
They can fly on their own,

And their hands, too, could be free
To fly away from wheeled wings.
The hands take their seed-bodies
To the door that leads
Nowhere, or to the brown loam-whirl
Where yellow flowers scattered.

Seeing

The deity with a thousand arms—
give or take a few
and an eye in each palm,
sits in a calm
corner of the art museum in Victoria
like a many-legged spider.
This god weaves through afternoon.

At the Butterfly Garden, there are many
captured gods. *Each butterfly eye
holds thousands of other eyes*, says the guide.
Trying to hide from predators' eyes,
some hang upside down under leaves,
still inside cone-shaped pupas
and quiet as Buddhas, while others are
flying flowers beholding me. Holding me.
Later, making love, I lower myself into one
of my lover's eyes, going spider-like down,
in a search for the kind of sight
multiple orgasms bring.
Each little wave blinks at me
as I go back on the ferry.

At home, my sculptor friend speaks of
her two lovers while the eyes in her fingertips
chip away at soapstone.
She creates three entwined figures
where once there was one.
Now six eyes look back at me from stone
while arms emerge, palms still hidden,
look inward.
This used to be Buddha, she laughs.

Summer Openings

In late July when clouds stop doing yoga poses,
begin to rise higher to become
white footprints in blue sand-sky
                   and then are erased by heatwave,
windows open around you.

They open to the spit and shove of motors.
They open to trampoline screams.
Memory smoke lifts
             and clears
to make way for the mint scents of friendships
so young or old you'd forgotten
                   you could see them
in the birch-leaf mirrors.

In mid-summer there is white noise
but there is also the cobalt blues.
                 A red scream
from a man you didn't know was
a drunk unleashes from inside his house
as you walk past with your little black shadow
to the echolalia
            of a beagle repeating the howl
of a wolf who lived centuries before.

Your own heat-struck voice
                 talking into the drainholes of a phone
comes back to you from a Quaker woman 150 years ago
as she first conceived your woman-rights.

In late July, open
              windows
give you a starfish voice from children
who become one child as they play games with the street.

One morning in the moment
when your summer lawn stops accepting
water for green blades of color,
                       a bright robin's call
pulls you to the kitchen-screen
                 just in time to see
life ripped
apart by a fledgling bigger than its offering mother
You're a little scared but you know
Your small patch of green
Holds the star-glisten of global seeds
                  As summer hovers,
Then begins to glide in every direction.

About the Author

Diane Averill's first book, *Branches Doubled Over With Fruit* (University of Florida Press) was a finalist for the 1991 Oregon Book Award, as was her second book, *Beautiful Obstacles* (Blue Light Press). In addition, she has had three chapbooks published.

Her work appears in many literary magazines and anthologies. In 2009, *Beautiful Obstacles* and her chapbook, *For All That Remains*, were chosen as part of a list of the best 150 books in Oregon.

Her work has been selected for Poetry in Motion, which puts poems on buses and light rail cars in the Portland Metropolitan area.

Diane is a graduate of the M.F.A. program at the University of Oregon where she won the annual award for the best poem by a graduate student. She taught in the English Department of Clackamas Community College from 1991 until she retired in 2010. She has been awarded an Oregon Literary Arts Fellowship.